HAL LEONARD FIDDLE METHOD BOOK 1

BY CHRIS WAGONER

ISBN 978-1-4234-2677-6

HAL•LEONARD® CORPORATION
7777 W. BLUEMOUND RD. P.O. BOX 13819 MILWAUKEE, WI 53213

In Australia Contact:
Hal Leonard Australia Pty. Ltd.
4 Lentara Court
Cheltenham, Victoria, 3192 Australia
Email: ausadmin@halleonard.com.au

Visit Hal Leonard Online at
www.halleonard.com

CONTENTS

ABOUT THE AUTHOR

Chris Wagoner has been an in-demand private instructor, performer, and session musician based in Madison, WI since 1984. He has co-founded several popular Midwest acts ranging from folk and jazz styles to blues and rock, and has appeared on numerous independent and major label releases as a multi-instrumentalist. To find out about Chris Wagoner's current musical projects and tour schedule, please visit **studiostrings.com**.

ACKNOWLEDGMENTS

Special thanks to all of my students, from whom I've learned so much, especially Bob Blackburn and Reid Gromnicki, who have challenged me to listen with new ears, and to my wife and long-time musical partner, Mary Gaines, who continues to inspire me; to all of my band-mates past and present; our parents, Don, Nancy, and Rose, who have supported our musical careers from day one; and special thanks also to Wil and Julie at Spruce Tree Music in Madison, WI, and Jake at Paradyme Productions.

ABOUT THIS BOOK

This book is written for the intermediate-beginner who may have some violin-playing experience already, has adequate music-reading skills and technique, but wants to begin exploring the fun art of fiddling. This book is also written as a primer for the advanced player who has had no experience with fiddling styles or techniques. Younger players may find it best to use this book with the help of an instructor, but adults should have no trouble negotiating this material on their own.

INTRODUCTION

A BRIEF HISTORY OF FIDDLING: THE ORAL TRADITION

The *fiddle*, or *violin*, is not native to the Americas. In case you were wondering (and don't feel bad, it's a very common question), the violin and the fiddle are the same instrument, but it will be most often referred to in this book as a *fiddle*. American fiddling draws on a vast repertoire of melodies, ranging back to the 17th century in United States and much earlier in Europe. Early fiddling traditions came to the U.S. with settlers from all over the European continent, as well as through the musical influence of black slaves from the African continent. Because of the predominance of early settlers from England, Ireland, and Scotland, the New England style of fiddling still bears those influences, and is famous for its driving dance rhythms.

In the 18th and 19th centuries, rural communities in the U.S. were isolated. News spread by word-of-mouth from travelers on foot, horseback, or boat. In the folk tradition, dance musicians were usually farmers or other trade-workers by day, and musicians by night—mostly entertaining themselves, family, and friends. Very few were full-time traveling musicians, so each community's ethnic musical traditions were rarely influenced by others—especially in more isolated locales. However, some regions along land trade routes or major rivers such as the Mississippi, the Ohio, and their tributaries, became melting pots of the traditions of travelers passing through or settling. This is one reason the Kentucky fiddle style is so rich and diverse, as well as other southern Appalachian styles. They borrow as much from the European traditions in the northern and eastern regions (such as Schottisches, Jigs, Reels, Hornpipes, and Marches), as they do from the slaves' field hollers ringing from the cotton fields.

Few folk musicians at that time knew how to read musical notation, so music was mostly passed on by aural tradition. Not surprisingly, a fiddler who learned a melody from a bagpiper probably would have picked up certain ways of phrasing, ornamentation (such as trills and grace notes), or special inflections (very similar to vocal accents or inflections) unique to the bagpipes. This special way of playing a particular melody was eventually passed on to the next musician who would add their unique history to it, and on and on. This is why there are almost as many versions of traditional melodies as there are players who play them. Today fiddlers often improvise variations on known melodies, and even compose their own tunes to add to the rich tradition. In contrast, in the European "classical" tradition, what the composer originally wrote is meant to be played in a similar way every time—by every musician. Of course, being human, musicians still manage to put their individual stamp on things, even when the rules are very strict.

STYLES

In the United States today there are several broad categories of folk music involving the fiddle: old-time, New England (which includes the Celtic-American tradition), French-Canadian, Texas, Western swing, blues, and Cajun. To limit this book to a reasonable scope, we will be focusing mainly on fiddle tunes and songs from the American old-time and Bluegrass traditions.

"Old-time," or "old-timey," is a rich collection of tunes and songs originating from the middle and Southern states, including the Appalachian region. These tunes tend to have more vocal-type inflections (such as slides) than the New England style. Bluegrass is a relatively modern tradition, popularly attributed to Bill Monroe, a prolific songwriter and masterful mandolinist active during the mid to late twentieth century. Bluegrass is a mix of Appalachian, old-timey, blues, and southern gospel music. Many bluegrass tunes are vocal or performance-oriented, and often have unusual forms that are not useful for dancing. Generally faster and more technically demanding than old-time, bluegrass fiddlers incorporate advanced bowing techniques, double-stops, and improvisational skills—all of which will be discussed later in the book.

YOUR FIDDLE AND BOW

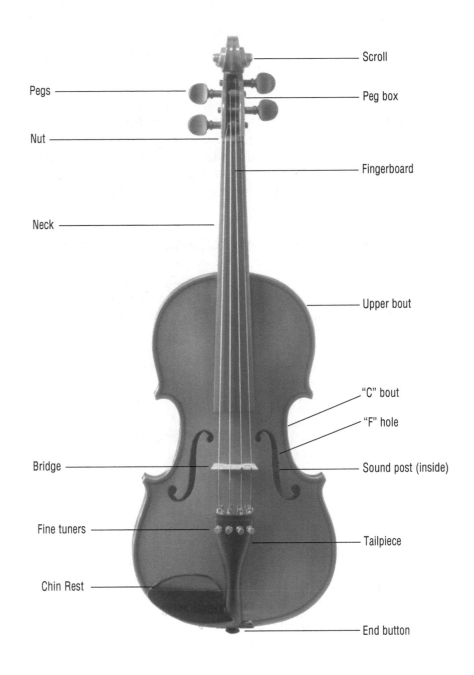

Scroll

Pegs

Peg box

Nut

Fingerboard

Neck

Upper bout

"C" bout

"F" hole

Bridge

Sound post (inside)

Fine tuners

Tailpiece

Chin Rest

End button

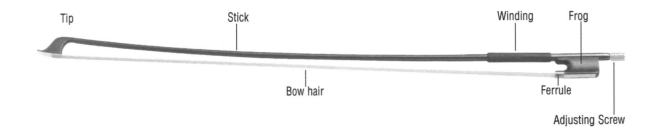

Tip

Stick

Winding

Frog

Bow hair

Ferrule

Adjusting Screw

PURCHASING AND RENTAL TIPS

Renting an instrument from a local music store is a good approach if you just want to try it out for awhile and see if fiddling is for you, however, if you are just starting out, give yourself at least six months of honest effort and be patient before deciding whether or not to continue! If you're thinking of investing at least a year into the pursuit of fiddling, you should consider purchasing a good "student package," including a "student model" violin, bow, and case. If taken care of, quality violins generally hold most of their resale value. It's generally a bad idea to buy instruments on the internet unless you know exactly what you're getting, or that it's from a reputable dealer. It's always best to see and handle the instrument you might be purchasing. "Student" packages are usually a good deal and are generally new instruments.

If you want to spend a little bit more and get a better sounding instrument, newer is not always better. Because of the violin's all-wood construction, the sound quality of the instrument tends to improve with age and playing as the wood "seasons." Look for cracks; seams that have opened up between the top or back and the sides of the violin are usually not a bad thing. As the wood expands with changes in temperature and humidity, the glue is meant to crack before the wood does, involving just a minor repair. Avoid any instrument with cracks on the neck, peg-box, or on the back or top (near the sound-post), unless you can be assured that it was repaired or could be repaired properly by a skilled *luthier* (a specialized stringed-instrument repair person).

The bridge should be flat, not warped, keeping in mind that the front of the bridge (facing the peg-box) is usually carved on a bevel, with the back of the bridge being flat and vertical.

The bow should be straight (except for their built-in camber) and somewhat stiff. Make sure the adjusting screw works properly for tightening and loosing the bow-hair. Don't worry about broken bow-hair—bows need to be rehaired periodically anyway, and it's not expensive.

If possible, have your newly purchased violin set up by a good luthier. In most cases, a good "set up" entails a sound-post and bridge adjustment (or replacement), an overall inspection, and a fresh set of strings (avoid steel strings—they're cheap, but loud and harsh-sounding).

And finally, don't scrimp on the case. It's best to buy a padded case that has a method of securing the instrument in the case by the neck so it doesn't bang around loosely. Also make sure the bow-holder securely holds the bow to prevent damage to both the violin and the bow while in the case.

INSTRUMENT CARE

The violin is held together by water-soluble glue called "hide" glue. Never leave your violin outside or in your car in extreme weather. Heat and cold can easily damage wood instruments and melt or crack the glue. If, for some reason, your violin is left out in extreme weather, bring it indoors and leave it in the case for an hour or two while the temperature gradually equalizes. It's the quick change in temperature when opening the case that can cause the most damage—from cracks in the finish to splits in the wood. Also, when wood gets dry, it cracks, so in northern climates during heating season use either a room humidifier or a case humidifer (you can purchase case humidifiers at most music stores that sell violins). To clean the rosin off the violin and bow, simply use a soft cloth. Never use alcohol as a cleaner—it will strip the soft finish. Also avoid violin polish that contains lemon oil, which can soften and damage the finish.

TUNING

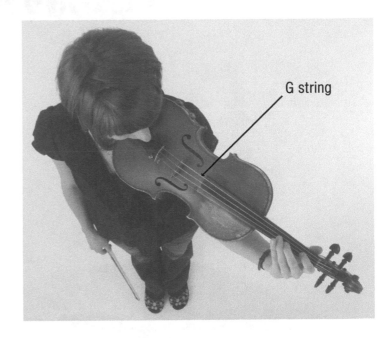

G string

When you are tuning your fiddle, you will adjust the pitch (highness or lowness of the sound) of each string by turning the corresponding *peg.* Tightening raises the pitch and loosening it lowers the pitch.

The strings are labeled in the following photo. The G string is the thickest/lowest string followed by D, A, and E. Fiddle players normally tune the A string first, followed by D. Next, the lowest string (G) is tuned followed by checking the A string again, then finally the top string (E). It is when tuning the top string that guitar and bass players will often tune along w/ the fiddle player since the guitar's lowest and highest strings are both E, and the bass' lowest string is an E.

TUNING TO A PIANO OR KEYBOARD

If you have an electronic keyboard or acoustic piano (that is relatively in-tune), tune the strings to the notes on the following diagram.

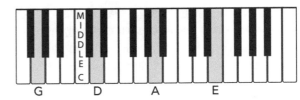

TUNING WITH AN ELECTRONIC TUNER

If you don't have an electronic keyboard or acoustic piano, or have trouble matching the pitches by ear, an electronic chromatic tuner is the way to go. A chromatic tuner recognizes all twelve unique pitches—naturals, sharps, and flats, so it will tell you exactly to what pitch your string is tuned. Avoid electronic "guitar" tuners that are not chromatic and are designed specifically to tune the strings of a guitar. Some electronic tuners also include a metronome, which is a handy practice tool.

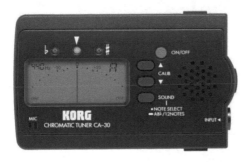

TUNING WITH A PITCH PIPE OR TUNING FORK

The two most portable tuners don't require batteries: a pitch pipe and a tuning fork. You can get a pitch pipe that has four pitches corresponding with the strings of a violin—not the most accurate tuning method, but quite common.

The tuning fork is the most accurate method, but one that requires a bit of practice to master. They are available for most pitches, but violinists typically use an A-440 tuning fork (meaning the A note that resonates at 440 cycles per second). To use it, simply hold it by the stem and strike the tines against a hard surface to make them vibrate. Touching the base of the stem against the top of the bridge or violin will amplify the pitch. Tune your A string to this pitch, then tune the other strings relative to the A string.

PLAYING POSITIONS

With your chin fully on the chin rest, the left shoulder should remain relaxed. The violin is held in place by the position of the head—there is no need to "pinch" the instrument between chin and shoulder. The neck of the violin should be angled out about 30 degrees from the left shoulder, with the body of the instrument tipped slightly so that the shoulder side is higher.

Note the position of the left-hand thumb and the way the violin is tipped forward.

The wrist is straight and fingers are curved, not flat.

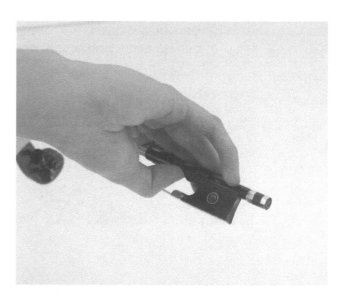

The thumb is bent, with the stick resting on the tip of the thumb. The fingers are curved and draping over the stick.

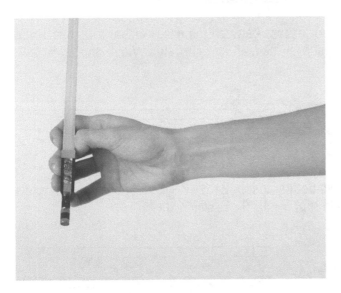

The bow hold should be very relaxed. Note the slight gap between fingers—just as there is when the hand is hanging at your side—completely relaxed. The middle finger is opposite the thumb, allowing the bow to pivot. The little finger should remain on top of the stick.

BOW HOLD: at the frog

The little finger is on top of the stick and quite bent, so that the wrist can remain straight. Notice that the stick has pivoted between the thumb and middle finger, allowing it to slide up the index finger a bit.

BOW HOLD: mid-bow

The stick is now right at the big knuckle of the index finger. Don't curl your fingers around to touch the frog. Other than the thumb and little finger, the fingertips don't need to touch the stick. Allow your fingers to drape over the stick in a relaxed manner.

BOW HOLD: at the tip

Now the little finger is much straighter, but still in contact with the stick. Notice that the bow is now pivoted so that the stick slides down the index finger closer to the hand.

MUSICAL SYMBOLS

Music is written in **notes** on a **staff**. The staff has five lines and four spaces between the lines. Where a note is written on the staff determines its **pitch** (highness or lowness). At the beginning of the staff is a **clef sign**. Violin and fiddle music is written in the treble clef.

Each line and space of the staff has a letter name. The **lines** are (from bottom to top) E - G - B - D - F, which you can remember as Every Good Beginner Does Fine. The **spaces** are, (from bottom to top) F - A - C - E, which spells "Face."

The staff is divided into several parts by bar lines. The space between two bar lines is called a **measure** (also known as a "bar"). To end a piece of music a double bar is placed on the staff.

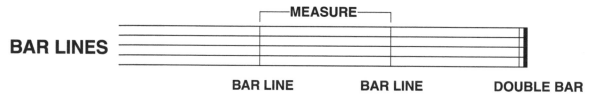

Each measure contains a group of **beats**. Beats are the steady pulse of music. You respond to the pulse or beat when you tap your foot.

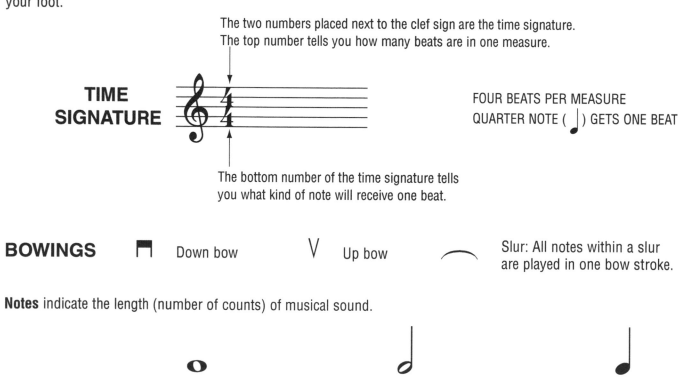

The two numbers placed next to the clef sign are the time signature. The top number tells you how many beats are in one measure.

TIME SIGNATURE

FOUR BEATS PER MEASURE
QUARTER NOTE (♩) GETS ONE BEAT

The bottom number of the time signature tells you what kind of note will receive one beat.

BOWINGS ⊓ Down bow   V Up bow   ⌣ Slur: All notes within a slur are played in one bow stroke.

Notes indicate the length (number of counts) of musical sound.

NOTES   WHOLE NOTE = 4 beats   HALF NOTE = 2 beats   QUARTER NOTE = 1 beat

When different kinds of notes are placed on different lines or spaces, you will know the pitch of the note and how long to play the sound.

SIMPLE MELODIES

Before we start playing, make sure you're in tune, following the instructions in the previous section.

We'll start with some simple melodies. Some will appear again later in the book as we explore new techniques. The difference between "fiddle tunes" and "songs" is that fiddle tunes are typically instrumental only, and feature the fiddle or some other instrument. Songs, no matter what their style, have lyrics and are meant to be sung. Learning a verse and chorus of lyrics is a fun way to help you memorize the melody and rhythm of a song, and it's never too soon to start memorizing! These first songs incorporate a simple back and forth bowing called "saw-bow."

In "Hot Corn, Cold Corn," notice the regular rhythm pattern that gives this tune it's danceable drive. Also pay attention to the *tie* on the last note (two or more notes can be "tied" together in one long bow-stroke, held for the duration of both notes).

HOT CORN, COLD CORN

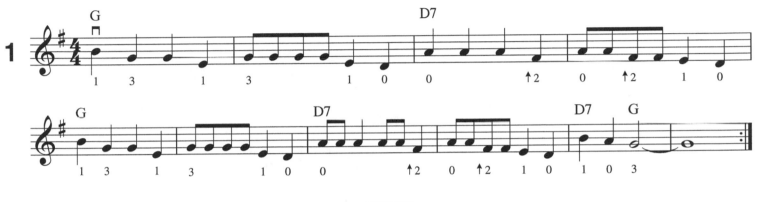

LYRICS

Verse 1:   Hot corn, cold corn, out in the kitchen, (3 times)
            Met an old cook jus a reelin' and a pitchin',
            Yes sir.

Verse 2:   All I want, to keep me happy,
            Is two little boys to call me pappy,
            One named Paul and one named Davey.
            One loves ham and the other loves gravy,
            Yes sir.

Chorus: Hot corn, cold corn, bring along your demijohn, (3 times)
            Fare thee well, my pretty gal, I'll meet you in the morning.
            Yes sir.

Here is one of many versions of "Cotton-Eyed Joe."

COTTON-EYED JOE

LYRICS

Verse 1:   If it hadn't a been for Cotton-Eye Joe,
            I'd have been married a long time ago,
            I'd have been married a long time ago.

Verse 2:   Where did you come from, where did you go?
            Where did you come from Cotton-Eye Joe?
            Where did you come from Cotton-Eye Joe?

The classic fiddle tune "Old Joe Clark" has two sections, called the "A" section and the "B" section. Most tunes have at least two parts. If both sections repeat, we say that the form is "AABB," or if the A part repeats but the B part does not, we say that it's form is "AAB." This version is only "AB."

OLD JOE CLARK

LYRICS

Verse 1:   Old Joe Clark he had a house, fifteen stories high,
           Every story in that house was filled with chicken pie.

Chorus: Round and round, old Joe Clark,
           Round and round I say.
           Round and round, old Joe Clark,
           'Til the break of day.

Verse 2:   Old Joe Clark he had a mule, his name was Morgan Brown,
           And every tooth in that mule's head was sixteen inches 'round.

The form of the next tune is also "AB."

CROW BLACK CHICKEN

LYRICS

Verse 1:   Chicken crow for midnight, chicken crow for day,
Along come an owl O Lord,
Toted that chicken away.

Chorus: Crow, black chicken, crow for day,
Crow, black chicken, fly away,
Crow, black chicken, crow for day.
I love chicken pie.

Verse 2:   I went on the mountain, I give my horn a blow,
I thought I heard my pretty gal say,
"Yonder comes my beau."

Repeat Chorus

ANGELINA BAKER

LYRICS

Verse 1:   Angelina Baker, lives on the village green,
The way that I love her beats all to be seen.

Chorus: Angelina Baker, Angelina Baker,
Angelina Baker, Angelina Baker.

Verse 2:   Angelina Baker, her age is 43,
I gave her candy by the peck, but she won't marry me.

Repeat Chorus

Verse 3:   The last time that I saw her, was at the county fair,
Her daddy chased me halfway home and told me to stay there.

Repeat Chorus

THE FEEL: STRAIGHT VS. SWING EIGHTH NOTES

This book is really all about "the feel"—how to make the music come alive, and make people want to dance, sing, cry, or maybe just smile. Perhaps the biggest difference between fiddling and playing the violin in a "classical" style has less to do with what notes you play than how you play them, or *articulation*. The next several chapters will focus on five key elements of articulation: swing, rhythm, slides, slurs, and anticipations.

STRAIGHT EIGHTHS VS. SWING EIGHTHS

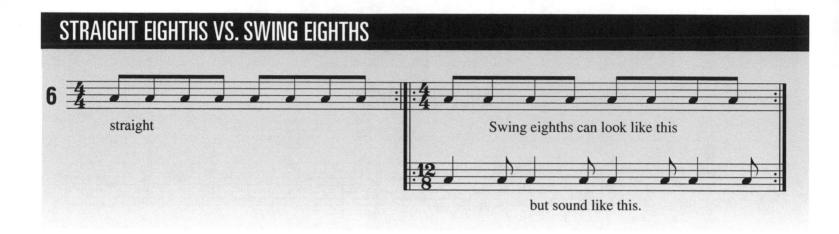

Try playing "Hot Corn, Cold Corn," first with "straight" eighth notes, then interpret the eighth notes with a swing rhythm.

SLIDES

The fiddle's singing tone is often compared to the human voice, but it is also similar to the voice in its unique ability to rise and fall smoothly from one pitch to another (unlike the piano, for instance, which is only capable of producing separate, distinct pitches). This smooth rising and falling is traditionally called a "glissando," but in the folk world is known as a "slide." Think about how the pitch of your voice rises and falls smoothly and naturally when you speak or sing. This is what we're trying to emulate with slides on the fiddle.

SLIDE PATTERNS

Try these slide patterns on all strings. The distance of a slide can range from less than a half-step to a whole step.

Sliding up from a pitch
Start on the written note and slide up from it, lightening the touch of your finger as you slide.

Sliding down from a pitch
Start on the written note and slide down from it, lightening the touch of your finger as you slide.

Sliding up to a pitch
Start with a light touch a half-step or whole step below the written note and slide up to it, adding full finger weight as you slide.

Hybrid Slides: "The Swell" (*rising and falling slide*)
Slide up from the written note, then back down to it.

The "Dip" (*falling and rising slide*)

Slide down from the written note, then back up to it.

"Rubin's Train" is a very bluesy tune that incorporates several different kinds of slides. Play it slowly so you can really feel all of the slides. Try it first without slides, and you will find that it lacks "the feel." Notice that the key signature has one flat, B♭. In this melody, try keeping your low first finger (the B♭) down, pivoting around it for all of the other notes and slides.

RUBIN'S TRAIN

SLURS

A *slur* connects two or more different pitches in a single bow-stroke.

Try slurring two notes, then four notes in a bow-stroke

"The Dawning of the Day" begins with a *pickup*, one or two notes that lead into the *down beat*, or the first beat of a tune. Pay close attention to bow markings and the fermata ⌒ sign over the quarter-note rest at the end of the third line. A *fermata* (often called a "birds-eye") lengthens a note or a rest just a bit longer than its normal value for dramatic effect.

THE DAWNING OF THE DAY

Here's a fun ragtime tune (usually just called a "rag") that incorporates a swing feel with slurs and ties that help keep the bowing pattern consistent.

STONE'S RAG

ANTICIPATIONS

Anticipations are notes that begin a quarter or eighth note before you expect them, often beginning on the last beat of a measure and tying into the down beat of the next measure. This gives a syncopated "off-beat" feel to the music and is most often used in old-timey dance music.

OLD JOE CLARK ("A" SECTION)

ANGELINA BAKER

CROW BLACK CHICKEN

BOWING TECHNIQUES

SHUFFLE BOWINGS

Shuffle bowings are repetitive rhythmic bowing patterns that help promote a driving, danceable feel. The first and most common is the "Nashville" shuffle, also called the "single" or "simple" shuffle.

Now try the Nashville shuffle with a moving line of eighth notes.

It is also common to accent beats 2 and 4 (called the "back beats"). This lends a driving "back-beat" feel to the shuffle.

"Fire on the Mountain" is a great tune for trying to figure out different shuffle patterns because it's quick to learn—the A and B sections are identical melodies, but played on different strings. The A section is in A major, and the B section is in D major. Also notice the "tag" ending, where the final phrase is repeated—in this case back in the original key. Because of the additional four-measure tag at the end of the form, this tune is not "square." A tune is "square" if it has two sixteen-measure parts (usually eight measures that are repeated): AABB. Square dancing gets its name from the even number of steps used in most of its dances.

Try "Fire on the Mountain" with a simple saw-bow pattern first (without the shuffle). Here is a short sample.

FIRE ON THE MOUNTAIN: SAW-BOW PATTERN

Now try it with the Nashville Shuffle.

FIRE ON THE MOUNTAIN: NASHVILLE SHUFFLE

Also know as "Bill Cheatham," this is a wonderful bluegrass standard that has several well-known variations. Here is a good Nashville shuffle version.

BILL CHEATEM

Another effective bowing pattern for fast reels in 4/4, 2/4, or cut-time is the "Georgia" shuffle (sometimes called the "double" shuffle). This pattern is most often used by bluegrass fiddlers when they really want to kick it into overdrive! It takes some getting used to, because each measure begins with an up-bow and the only down-bows are on the off-beats (beats 2 and 4)—ALL of the other eighth notes are slurred up-bows. Because there is only one eighth-note down-bow for every three eighth-note slurred up-bows, you need to push the bow faster on the down-bow, and the resulting accent will produce an even stronger back-beat.

Try the Georgia shuffle with a one-octave A major scale.

THE "GEORGIA" SHUFFLE

Next, try it out on "Fire on the Mountain."

FIRE ON THE MOUNTAIN: GEORGIA SHUFFLE

Play only
when repeating
to the beginning

CIRCLE BOWING

Circle bowing is a repetitious back and forth saw-bow movement between adjacent strings in which the bow-hand moves in a circular motion. This bowing is often used in fiddle tunes, so it's important to know how to do it correctly.

To practice this motion, begin by resting the bow equally on the D and A strings. Your elbow and upper arm should be parallel to the bow.

Start drawing medium-length bow-strokes, playing both strings with equal weight. Concentrate on the even line your bow-hand is drawing in the air. Gradually turn that flat stroke into a very shallow and long oval until you're playing separate strokes, alternating between each string. Be sure to keep your upper arm still—rotate from the elbow only!

Pick up the tempo gradually while shortening your bow-stroke and turning the oval into a successively smaller circle. Remember—the faster you go, the shorter the bow.

"Soldier's Joy" is a very old tune from the British Isles that is often played for dances due to its strong propelling beat and memorable melody. This is also a good example of a melody dictating the best bowing to use—in this case, the circle bowing.

Try the following simple melody first to get a feel for the basic tune.

SOLDIER'S JOY (SIMPLE VERSION)

Here are some exercises based on the melody. Notice how the added slur simplifies the bowing pattern, making the string crossing smoother, and the strong beats even stronger.

STANDARD BOWING EXERCISE

CIRCLE BOWING EXERCISE

Now try the more advanced version of "Soldier's Joy" with circle bowing. If you try the Nashville shuffle on the A section, you'll quickly find yourself finger-tied! On the B section, try to keep your left-hand fingers down.

SOLDIER'S JOY (CIRCLE BOWING VERSION)

Play only
when repeating
to the beginning

"Harvest Home" is also a popular tune from the British Isles, and is often played as a "hornpipe." *Hornpipes* are usually played slower than reels and feature a very pronounced dotted rhythm, even though they may be written as "straight" eighth notes.

HARVEST HOME

A variation of the circle bowing is what may be called "half-circle" bowing, in which the bow dips toward the upper adjacent string but never leaves the lower string of the pair.

HALF-CIRCLE BOWING

HEMIOLA BOWING

Another interesting bowing pattern involves a *hemiola*—a rhythmic figure that creates the illusion of being in a different time signature, usually by grouping three notes of a four-note pattern.

HEMIOLA BOWING

Try this ear-twister!

ALTERNATING BOWING PATTERNS

Here is a version of "Old Joe Clark" that incorporates both half-circle and hemiola bowing patterns.

OLD JOE CLARK

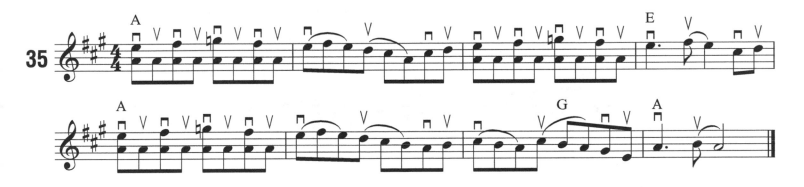

This next example is a fairly advanced tune that's often requested. Remember to leave the fingers down where specified. In the second measure, place your first finger equally between both strings without letting the knuckle collapse.

DEVIL'S DREAM BOWING EXERCISE

In the following version of "Devil's Dream," the A section alternates between a Nashville shuffle and circle bowing, but the B section is mostly circle bowing.

DEVIL'S DREAM

Next, try the A section of "Devil's Dream" with the Georgia Shuffle.

DEVIL'S DREAM (WITH GEORGIA SHUFFLE)

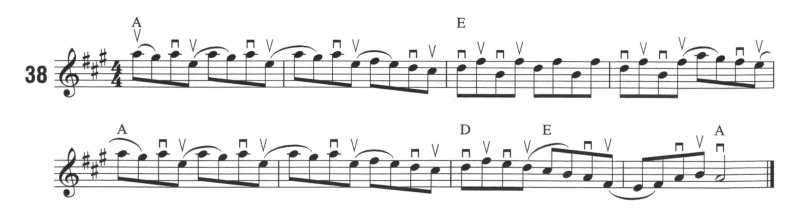

PRACTICAL MUSIC THEORY: THE UNIVERSAL LANGUAGE

Music is often called the "universal language." One reason is that the world shares a common music notation system, but another more important reason is that music has the power to move us emotionally. Music from other countries may sound foreign, but it can still convey a message, a story, and an emotion—from the pinnacle of joy to the depths of sorrow. But music is also a language in the same way our spoken languages are. Both use complex rhythms, rising and falling pitches, and subtle tonal shapes and articulations to communicate. Each also has rules of order that are essential to communication. In our spoken language this is called "grammar" and "syntax," and in the language of music it's called "music theory." The more you know about how a language is constructed, the better you will be able to communicate. In the next chapter, we will explore some key music theory concepts that apply directly to fiddling.

SCALES AND MODES

INTERVALS

An *interval* is the distance between any two notes or pitches, with a *half step* being the smallest interval (G to G♯ is an example of a half step). One *whole step* equals two half steps (G to A is a whole-step).

39

Memorize the intervals up to an octave.

40

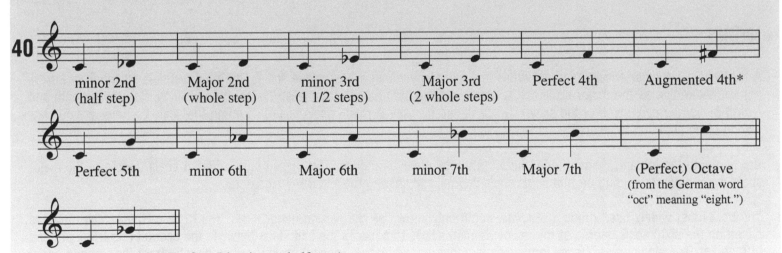

*diminished 5th(Perfect 5th minus a half-step)
The diminished 5th sounds the same as an augmented 4th.

SCALES

A *scale* is an ascending or descending sequence of pitches that are ordered consecutively from A to G, then starting over again with A. (A, B, C, D, E, F, G, A).

First, play the familiar D major scale, shown in the next example.

D MAJOR SCALE

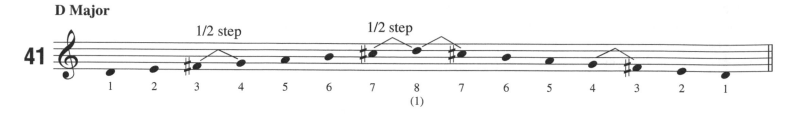

Next, play a one-octave E major scale, counting the steps again. Notice how your finger position (and the key signature) must change to accommodate the pattern of whole and half steps of the major scale relative to your new *tonic* (first note of the scale).

E MAJOR SCALE

MODES

A *mode* is a particular arrangement of whole and half steps within a one-octave scale. The most well-known mode is *Ionian*, commonly known as the major scale. Its sound is defined by a half step between the third and fourth, and the seventh and eighth *scale degrees* (steps of the scale). Go back and play the D major scale again, counting the scale degrees as you play, paying close attention to where the half-steps fall.

Starting with the Ionian (Major) mode, there are a total of seven modes, each based on a different scale degree of the major scale, beginning and ending on that same scale degree, and sharing the same key signature.

The next most widely used mode is *Aeolian*, commonly known as the natural minor scale. The tonic of the Aeolian mode is based on the sixth scale degree of the major (Ionian) scale. This places the half steps between the second and third, and the fifth and sixth scale degrees. Notice in the example that the E minor (E Aeolian) scale is pulled directly from the G major scale, so they share the same key signature. We call these scales "relative" to each other. E minor is the relative minor to G major.

G MAJOR SCALE (IONIAN) AND E MINOR SCALE (AEOLIAN)

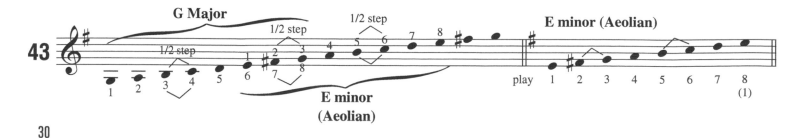

The other two common modes used in fiddling are *Dorian* (based on the second scale degree of the major scale) and *Mixolydian* (based on the fifth scale degree of the Major scale). Since you've played "Old Joe Clark," you've already encountered the Mixolydian mode!

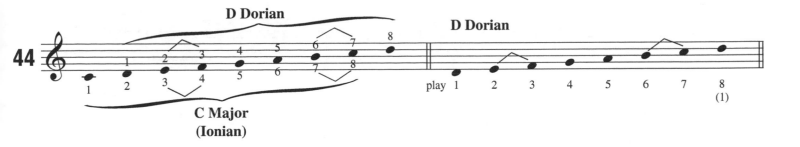

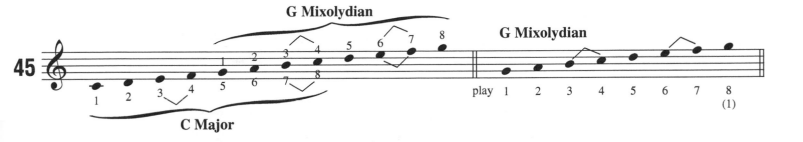

Now do a side-by-side comparison of these four common modes by starting each on the same tonic.

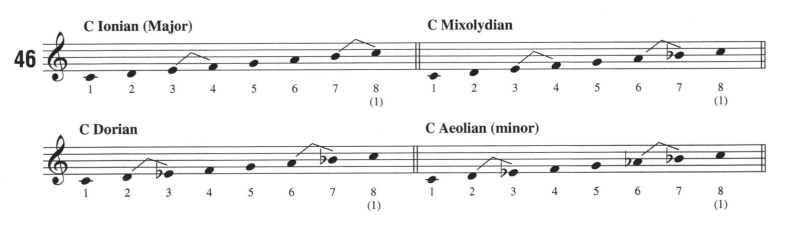

The next tune, "Hobart's Transformation" is based on the A Dorian mode. The key signature indicates G major, but the tonic of the tune is A. Thus A Dorian uses the same notes as the G major scale, but is ordered from A up to A.

HOBART'S TRANSFORMATION (A DORIAN)

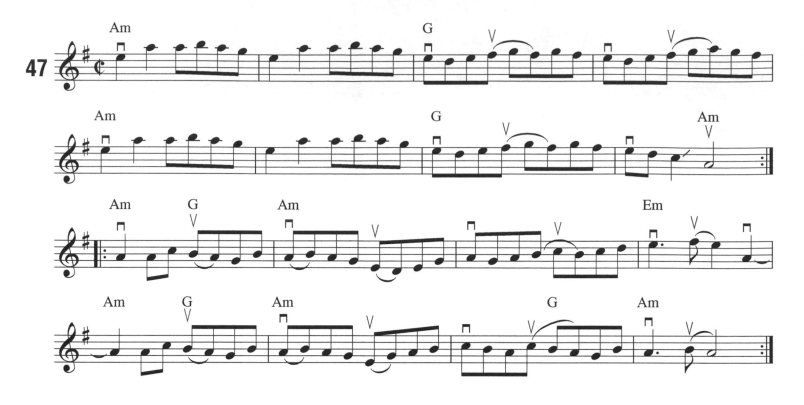

A *Jig* is an Irish dance set in 6/8 time. Typically the first eighth note of each group of three is held a bit longer, for a slightly loping swingy feel.

"Banish Misfortune" is a three-part tune, with A, B, and C sections.

BANISH MISFORTUNE (D MIXOLYDIAN)

PENTATONIC SCALES

From the Latin word, "penta," meaning "five," a *pentatonic scale* uses only five notes, not counting the octave.

Minor Pentatonic
The *minor pentatonic scale* is sometimes called the "blues" scale, and is derived from the minor (Aeolian) mode by omitting the second and sixth scale degrees.

E MINOR PENTATONIC

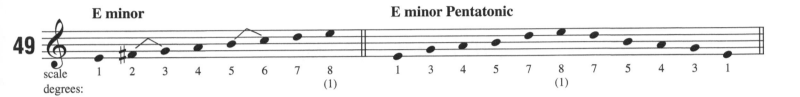

E MINOR PENTATONIC—EXTENDED

2 octave E minor Pentatonic scale extending down to A and up to B.

In the next example, notice how the finger patterns of one-octave sections of pentatonic scales are symmetrical.
In "Poor Wayfaring Stranger," notice how slides accentuate the "bluesy" quality of the tune.

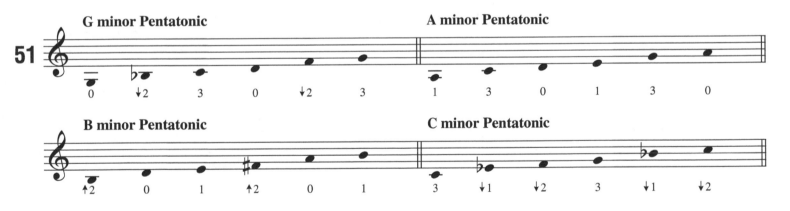

POOR WAYFARING STRANGER

Major Pentatonic

The *major pentatonic* scale is derived from the major (Ionian) mode by omitting the fourth and seventh scale degrees.

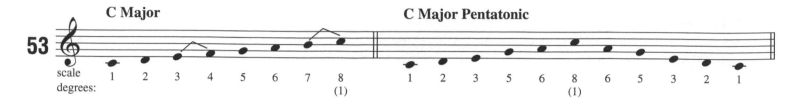

53

C Major   C Major Pentatonic

scale degrees: 1   2   3   4   5   6   7   8 (1)   1   2   3   5   6   8 (1)   6   5   3   2   1

BILLY IN THE LOWGROUND

54

34

SEQUENCES

Learning to break scales up into *sequences* (melodic patterns that repeat, but start on a different pitch each time) is an essential skill players use when composing a new tune or variation, or when *improvising* (making it up as you go). Play as written, but also try continuing the sequences up one octave.

G MAJOR SEQUENCES

55

56

57

BLACKBERRY BLOSSOM

Here are a couple of variations on the A section of "Blackberry Blossom."

Now try some cool-sounding pentatonic sequences. Blues and rock musicians often use these patterns, but they show up in bluegrass and old-timey styles as well.

A MINOR PENTATONIC SEQUENCES

VARIATIONS

VARIATION TYPES

One of the great joys of fiddling is the freedom of expression this type of music allows. Established fiddlers almost always have their own versions of tunes that are borrowed from bits and pieces of other tunes they've learned over many years. Sometimes changes to tunes happen naturally over time, and sometimes variations are deliberately created. There are three main types of variations:

1. **Rhythmic**—the melody remains basically the same, but rhythms and bowing patterns are altered.

2. **Melodic**—rhythms may remain unchanged while certain melody notes or phrases are altered.

3. **Stylistic**—both melody and rhythm may be altered to change the overall style of a tune.

Here are two very different versions of "Cotton-Eyed Joe," where both the rhythm and melody have been altered.

COTTON-EYED JOE I

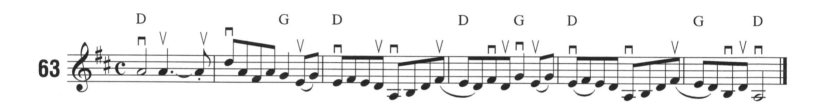

COTTON-EYED JOE II

"Red-Haired Boy" (also known as "The Little Beggar Boy") is a classic example of a traditional Irish tune that has also found its way into the standard old-timey and Bluegrass repertoire.

RED-HAIRED BOY I

RED-HAIRED BOY II

CONSTRUCTING A "BREAK"

One method of constructing a fiddle "break," or "breakdown" for a song with a simple melody is by first identifying the most important or strongest melody notes or "target notes" (often the down beat of each measure, as circled in "Worried Man Blues"). Using scales based on the chords, or a pentatonic scale based on the mode of the song, construct a melodic line mostly of eighth-notes that connects the previously *targeted notes*.

WORRIED MAN BLUES

It takes a wor-ried man to sing a wor-ried song, It takes a wor-ried

man to sing a wor-ried song, It takes a wor-ried man to sing a wor-ried

song I'm wor-ried now but I won't be wor-ried ___ long. ___

Note: Circled notes are target notes.

Use the notes of the G major pentatonic scale to construct a break.

G MAJOR PENTATONIC SCALE

G Major Pentatonic Scale

The next example shows a fiddle break incorporating the target notes.

FIDDLE BREAK

TRIADS AND ARPEGGIOS

Whenever we play two or more notes simultaneously we are playing "chords," just like when a guitar player grabs a fist full of notes and strums the strings, or a piano player spreads their fingers and plays a bunch of notes at the same time. When we play *double-stops* (two notes at the same time) we are creating chords. The most basic chord is called a "triad." As the name implies, a triad is made up of three notes. In its most basic form, called "root position," the three notes are stacked in intervals of thirds (line–line–line, or space–space–space). When a triad is in root position, the bottom note is called the "root," and the chord is named by its root note.

TRIADS IN ROOT POSITION

Examples of triads in root position

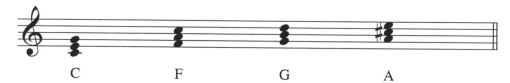

If we invert a root position triad by moving the root up an octave, we get the same chord, but it is now "voiced" differently—meaning that the notes are now in different positions (C, E, G to E, G, C). This new voicing is called the "first inversion." The root of this triad is still C, but it's no longer the bottom note. The third of the chord is now on the bottom and the triad is no longer stacked in intervals of thirds. If we now move the new bottom note up an octave (E, G, C to G, C, E), we call this the "second inversion." If we repeat this process one more time, we're back to a root-position C triad, but up an octave from its original root position voicing.

Inversions of a C Major triad

71

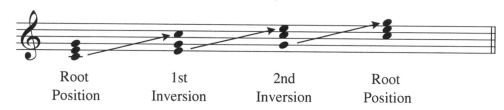

One of the most important concepts to understand in music theory is that once we've defined what notes make up a certain chord, it doesn't matter in which octave or order you play them—it's still the same chord.

It's very useful to memorize the sequence of notes in each triad:

72

A – C – E
B – D – F
C – E – G
D – F – A
E – G – B
F – A – C
G – B – D

Obviously we can't play most full triads on the fiddle, so we need to voice them in ways that are playable. One way of expressing these chords on the fiddle is by playing the notes of the chords separately—this is called an *arpeggio.*

D MAJOR TRIAD AND ARPEGGIO

D major Triad and Arpeggio

73

Triad (listen)   Play the arpeggio

"Soldier's Joy" is a good example of a very arpeggiated melody. Turn back to the first version of "Soldier's Joy" and see if you can identify how the chords written above the melody relate to the arpeggios in the melody (notice that the first measure is a D Major arpeggio in root position).

"Fisher's Hornpipe" is another good example of an arpeggiated melody. Notice that the opening phrase in the B section is the same as the beginning of "Soldier's Joy."

FISHER'S HORNPIPE

74

INTROS, OUTROS, AND "TAG" ENDINGS

Now that you have a few tunes under your belt, you need to learn how to start them—so that those you're playing with know when to begin—this is called a "kick-off" or "intro." Instead of counting out loud, the fiddler or guitarist usually plays a rhythmic pattern for a measure or two to communicate the tempo to the rest of the band and dancers. The most common intro is called "potatoes," or "taters." Here is an example of a two-measure intro in the key of D Major (four "taters").

FOUR TATERS

Another simple intro involves accented down-bows at the frog. Start with the bow above the strings and land right under your bow-hand, making a circle in the air as you lift the bow between each stroke. Here is an example in the key of A Major.

ACCENTED DOWNBOWS

We also need a good way to end tunes, and this section is sometimes called an "outro." Typically at dances, the fiddler raises his/her foot to signal the band that the tune is about to end. It's perfectly fine to just end a tune with the final note of the melody, but another exciting way to end is with a "tag." A tag ending is an additional measure or two (or more) "tagged" onto the end of a song. Tags often repeat the last measure or two of the melody, or are one of several standard tags.

The following shows a few examples of some standard tag endings. Number one is a fun old tag which can be a bit corny, but good to know. It's a strong ending because it begins and ends on the tonic. Number three is a descending major pentatonic sequence.

STANDARD TAGS

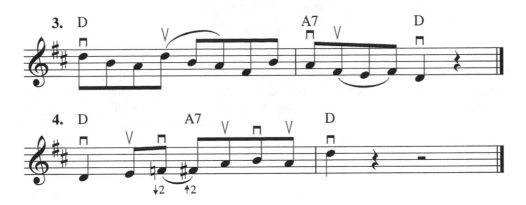

Try stringing two tags together to make a double tag. It sounds best if you use two tags with slightly different rhythms or whose melodies move in different directions.

The final tag is a double tag consisting of four measures (or two sets of two).

DOUBLE TAG

DRONES

One of the sounds that sets fiddling apart from playing in a conventional "classical" manner is the use of a technique called *Bariolage*—more commonly referred to in the fiddling world as "droning." Bariolage involves playing a moving passage of notes simultaneously with a static, or non-moving note—often an adjacent open string (depending on the key of the tune). Remember that playing two notes at once is also called a "double-stop." Some triple-stops are also possible. Knowing what notes are in a triad or chord is essential to knowing which open string or fingered notes can be droned along with a melody. Because the notes of a D major chord are D, F#, and A, our open-string drone choices are D or A during the measures supported by a D chord.

"Angelina Baker" (key of D major) is a good tune with which to practice using drone strings because in this melody, the drone is always the open string below the melody.

ANGELINA BAKER

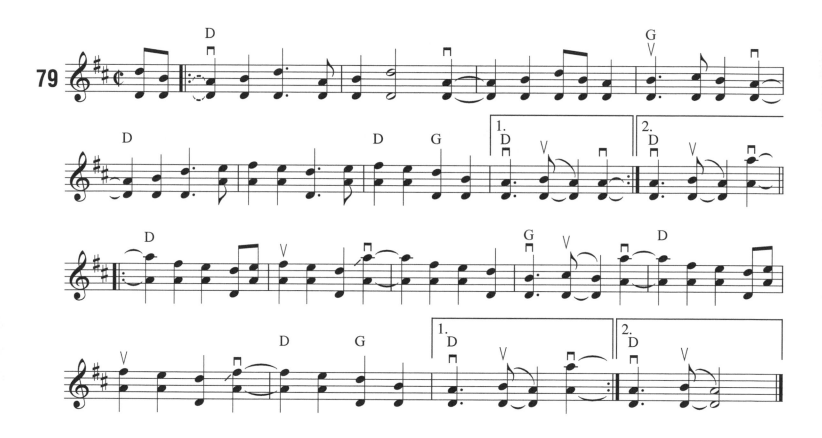

"Crow Black Chicken" is in the key of G major, another good one for drones.

CROW BLACK CHICKEN

Not only is the form of "Tater Patch" AAB, but the B section is twelve measures long—a very un-square tune! The simple saw bowing really drives it, and the frequent use of non-chord tones gives this tune a very unusual sound.

TATER PATCH

PLAYING "BACKUP"

By now you've learned several popular fiddle tunes along with techniques to help bring them to life. But playing a learned melody is only half the experience of playing with others. When not playing the melody, or "lead," you will need to learn how to play an *accompaniment* part, called "playing backup," while another instrument or vocalist takes the lead (or melody). You will be part of the rhythm section—the musicians who provide the chordal and rhythmic foundation that supports the song.

BACKUP CHORDS

Any two notes of a triad will effectively represent that chord. Let's break down a two-octave G major arpeggio (representing a G major chord) into all of the different possible double-stop chord combinations. When we do this for all of the chords in a tune, we can start to make melodic choices about how best to get from one chord to the next.

G MAJOR ARPEGGIO AND DOUBLE-STOPS

Now let's use the same process to figure out double-stop combinations for the other chords in our practice tune, "Angelina Baker."

A MAJOR ARPEGGIO AND DOUBLE-STOPS

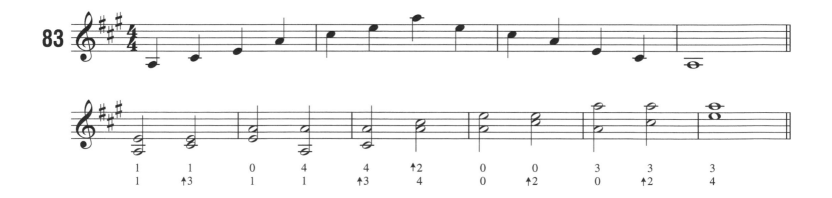

D MAJOR ARPEGGIO AND DOUBLE-STOPS

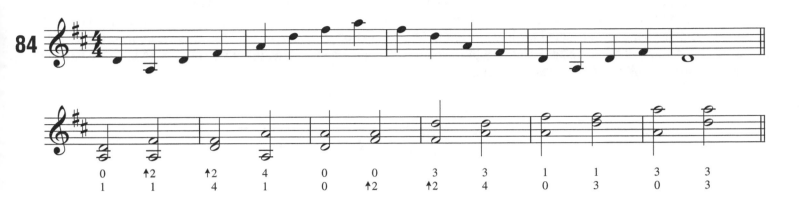

Along with playing chords, another important aspect of playing backup is providing rhythmic support similar to what the guitar, mandolin, bass, and even drums might do in an ensemble. Try these different rhythm patterns with the following chord voicings on "Angelina Baker."

LONG-BOW CHORDING

This technique can be highly effective on Celtic tunes or to alternate with other patterns. You can make long-bow backup more interesting by occasionally throwing in some shorter bow-strokes.

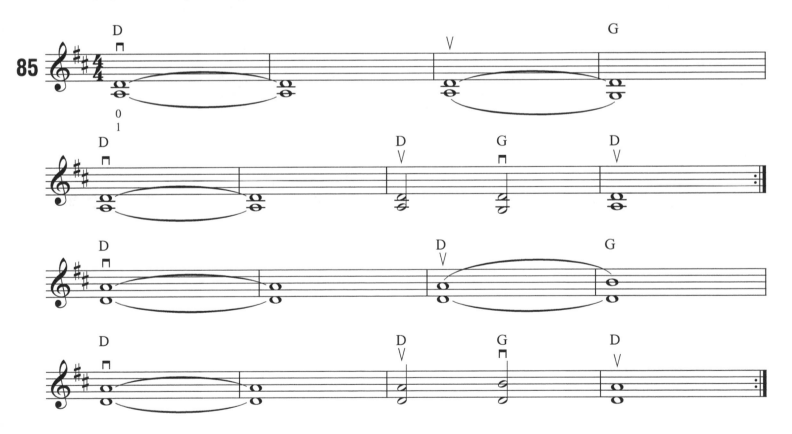

THE CHOP

The *chop* is the most common and effective rhythm style for medium to up-tempo bluegrass and old-timey tunes in 4/4, 2/4, or cut-time signatures. It imitates the role of the mandolin in a bluegrass groups by "chopping" on the second and fourth beat of the measure—either short accented down-bows at the frog for a stronger sound or ricocheted up-bows near the tip for a softer touch. The chords to "Angelina Baker" are the same for both the A and B parts, but try one part with up bows near the tip, and the next part with down strokes at the frog.

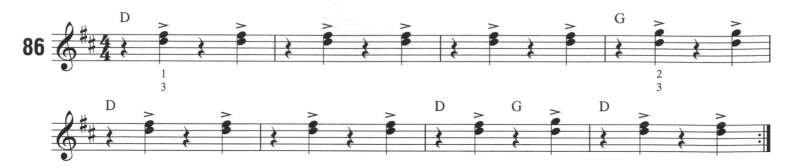

ACCENTED SHUFFLES

Because the accent pattern can be easily shifted and manipulated while playing eighth notes, this can be one of the most versatile and interesting forms of backup rhythm. De-emphasize all unaccented notes by playing them with a very short bow-stroke. This will help emphasize the accented notes even more. Watch out for the different pattern in the last two measures.

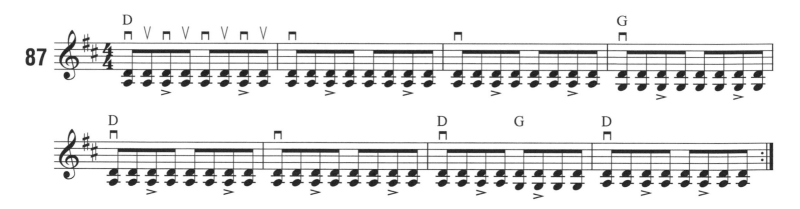

CROSS-TUNING

Cross-tuning is the art of using alternate tunings other than the traditional "G-D-A-E" to create different melodic or chordal possibilities. Many cross-tunings involve tuning at least two strings in octaves, creating a beautiful sympathetic resonance. As you can imagine, some cross-tunings may radically alter the usual fingering patterns. Let's start out with some simpler tunings that won't alter the usual fingerings, but will create that unique ringing resonance.

For the following two tunes, tune your G string up one whole step to an A (it should sound one-octave below the open A string). Finger as written, only using the low A as a drone.

ARKANSAS TRAVELER
(A-D-A-E)

Try this crazy chromatic variation of the ending lick—replacing the last two measures of the A and B sections.

ENDING "LICK" VARIATION

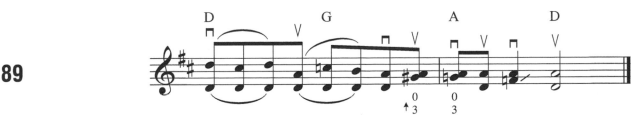

Here's a fun novelty tune that incorporates left hand *pizzicato* (denoted by the "+" to be played by plucking with the little finger of your left hand). Tune both your G and D strings up one whole step. This very resonant tuning has two sets of strings tuned in octaves. Finger as written.

CLUCK OLD HEN
(A-E-A-E)

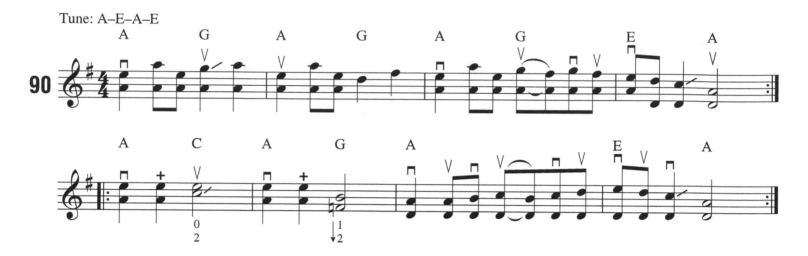

ADVANCED TUNES

Originally this was a fiddle tune played for dances. Lyrics were later added that incorporated a fun "call and response." Compare the simpler vocal version with the instrumental break that happens between the verses.

SAIL AWAY LADIES

91

Ev-er I get my new house done, sail a-way la-dies sail a-way. Give my old one to my son,

sail a-way la-dies sail a-way. Don't she rock 'em die - dee-o, don't __ she rock 'em

die - dee-o, don't __ she rock 'em die - dee-o, don't __ she rock 'em die - dee-o.

Verse 2:
    (Solo) Children don't you grieve and cry,
    (All)   Sail away ladies, sail away.
    (Solo) You'll be angels by and by,
    (All)   Sail away ladies, sail away.

Instrumental Break

Here's our old favorite, all dressed up! This advanced version of "Old Joe Clark" incorporates half-circle bowing. Remember that your bow-hand should make a short circle or oval pattern in the air, but keep contact with the A string on both the up and down bow strokes. This tune also works well cross-tuned to A–D–A–E (G string up a whole step to A), and you don't even need to alter your fingering!

OLD JOE CLARK (WITH "OLD-TIMEY" SHUFFLE)

Try the single-note practice version of "Jolie Blon" to get a feel for the melody and "cajun-shuffle" waltz bowing before attempting the advanced double-stop version. D.C. al Coda means "go back to the beginning (D.C. stands for da capo, "the beginning") and play until the Coda sign, then jump to the Coda. The form of this tune is AAB, but the last time through play two more A's and end with the Coda. A slight accent on the second and third beats of each measure (when possible) will give this tune the right feel.

JOLIE BLON (SINGLE-NOTE VERSION)

JOLIE BLON (A CAJUN WALTZ—ADVANCED VERSION)

Keep practicing, play as much as possible with other people, and listen to as many recordings as you can get your hands on. Now you're a fiddler—enjoy!